About the photographer

Michael Poliza is a Marco Polo of the New Millennium.
As a young entrepreneur he introduced Germany to the digital world, and more recently undertook a thousand-day journey around the globe in search of the most beautiful and endangered places, following the trails of the old-time explorers.

But backpacks and travelers' checks were not for him. Instead, he filled a custom-built boat to the scuppers with the latest technologies and media, and used his visionary business savvy to get funding from prominent international sponsors. A book and DVD chronicling this unique journey have revealed the world in a whole new way to tens of thousands of people.

After selling the boat that had been his home for three years, Poliza then undertook a mental journey around the globe, contemplating the most fascinating, beautiful and exciting place to use as a base for further travel. Though he was intimately acquainted with many regions that would fit the bill, he finally settled on Southern Africa. This book is a testament to the wisdom of that choice.

Through this rich collection of his magnificent images, he takes us on our own journey of discovery into the mysterious and magical continent of Africa. If only there were more men like Michael Poliza in the world ...

Florian Langenscheidt

Journeys of Discovery

In 2000 I started to get emails from a vessel called "STARSHIP" that was cruising the world on a three-year environmental awareness expedition, saying that some of the crew would like to visit some of the best wildlife areas in southern Africa.

On that first safari I arranged for Michael Poliza and some of his crew to visit the Okavango Delta in Botswana. Instantly he fell under the spell of this wonderful country, its wildlife and people. The connection was made. Michael came to see me after he finished the project and we started on a journey of discovery together. I was bringing him to some of the planet's wildest and most intriguing wildlife areas—and he was easing us techno-dinosaurs into the world of digital photography and technology.

Michael brought a new perspective into wildlife photography and managed to photograph many animals in a way that departed from the general rules of wildlife photography. For example, he caught all the essence of the majestic Lion King in a close-up image, yet he broke the rules by not showing the eyes.

He captured the essence of these wonderful areas and amazing wildlife in his very own style. He brought a new, more artistic view into wildlife photography. Many of his images portray an animal in a way that I had never seen before. A different angle, extremely close or very graphical, often waiting for hours and days to get that special shot. And he never seemed to get tired of trying and trying again, believing that there is always a better shot out there.

Michael has inspired many of our guides, staff and guests to become better photographers. And he has inspired us as a company to go further and better.

Colin Bell

Über den Fotografen

Michael Poliza ist ein Marco Polo unserer Jahrtausendwende.

Erst erschloss er als Unternehmer Deutschland den digitalen Welten. Dann ging er selbst tausend Tage lang auf Weltreise – auf der Suche nach den schönsten und gefährdetsten Stellen dieser Erde und auf den Spuren der alten Entdecker.

Aber nicht mit Rucksack und Reiseschecks, sondern mit einem eigens konstruierten Schiff bis zur Halskrause voll von Technik und Medien. Und mit vernünftigem wirtschaftlichem Sachverstand, d.h. finanziert über große Sponsoren aus der ganzen Welt. Buch und DVD über diese einzigartige Reise erschlossen Zehntausenden die Welt ganz neu.

Dann ging er im Kopf um die ganze Welt und überlegte, wo es am schönsten und besten und spannendsten für ihn werden könnte nach dem Verkauf des Schiffes. Und er, der wahrlich alles kannte, entschied sich schnell für den Süden Afrikas. Das hat er nie bereut.

Und nun erschließt er uns in vorliegendem Prachtband diesen geheimnisvollen und magischen Kontinent neu mit großartigen Bildern. Danke dafür! Schade, dass es nicht mehr Polizas auf dieser Welt gibt!

Florian Langenscheidt

Florian Langenscheidt, Gesellschafter der Langenscheidt-Verlagsgruppe und Autor zahlreicher Bücher, ist Stiftungsratsmitglied des World-Wide Fund for Nature (WWF) und Mitglied des Chairman's Council am Museum of Modern Art in New York.

Entdeckungsreisen

Im Jahr 2000 erhielt ich eine Reihe von E-Mails von einem Schiff namens „STARSHIP", das sich auf einer dreijährigen Expeditionsfahrt rund um die Welt befand, die im Zeichen des Umweltbewusstseins stand. Sie schrieben, dass einige der Crew gern ein paar der schönsten Wildparks des südlichen Afrikas besuchen wollten.

Auf unserer ersten Safari arrangierte ich für Michael Poliza und einen Teil seiner Crew einen Besuch im Okavango-Delta in Botswana. Augenblicklich stand er unter dem Bann dieses wunderbaren Landes, seiner Tierwelt und seiner Menschen. Die Verbindung war hergestellt. Michael besuchte mich nach Beendigung seines Projekts in meinem Büro, und wir gingen gemeinsam auf Entdeckungsreise. Ich führte ihn zu einigen der unberührtesten und faszinierendsten Plätze auf diesem Planeten – und er brachte uns technischen Hinterwäldlern die Welt der digitalen Fotografie und Technologie nahe.

Michael brachte eine neue Perspektive in die Fotografie von wilden Tieren. Viele seiner Tierbilder lassen die allgemeinen Regeln der Wildlife-Fotografie hinter sich. Er schaffte es beispielsweise, das ganze Wesen des majestätischen Königs der Löwen in einer Nahaufnahme einzufangen, auch wenn er dabei die Regeln brach und die Augen nicht zeigte.

Er hat das Wesen dieser herrlichen Landschaften und ihrer überwältigenden Tierwelt in einem sehr eigenen Stil eingefangen. Mit ihm ist eine neue, mehr künstlerische Sicht in die Fotografie von Wildtieren gekommen. Viele seiner Bilder porträtieren Tiere in einer Weise, wie ich es nie zuvor gesehen habe. Ein anderer Winkel, extrem nah oder sehr grafisch fotografiert – oft musste er stundenlang warten, um genau dieses bestimmte Bild zu bekommen. Nie schien er müde zu werden, es wieder und immer wieder zu versuchen, in der Überzeugung, dass da draußen ein noch besseres Bild für ihn zu holen sein musste.

Michael hat viele unserer Führer, Angestellten und Besucher dazu inspiriert, bessere Fotografen zu werden. Und er hat uns als Unternehmen dazu inspiriert, weiterzugehen und besser zu werden.

Colin Bell

Colin Bell ist ein echter Pionier der afrikanischen Safari-Industrie und Umweltschützer aus Überzeugung. Mit seinen Wilderness Safaris Camps kam eine neue Qualität in das Safari-Erlebnis in Afrika. Im Namen des Teams von Wilderness Safaris nahm er viele der renommiertesten Umweltpreise entgegen, bevor er sich Anfang 2006 neuen Aufgaben stellte.

Le photographe

Michael Poliza est l'un des Marco Polo du tournant de ce siècle.

Entrepreneur, il a ouvert l'Allemagne au monde numérique. Puis il a lui-même parcouru le monde pendant mille jours – à la recherche des endroits les plus beaux et les plus menacés de cette planète et sur les traces des anciens explorateurs.

Sans sac à dos ni chèques de voyage, mais à bord d'un bateau construit spécialement à cet effet, bourré de technique et de médias. Et avec une grande intelligence de l'aspect économique, puisque financé par de grands sponsors du monde entier. Le livre et le DVD relatant ce voyage exceptionnel ont permis à des milliers de personnes de découvrir le monde avec un regard nouveau.

Ensuite, il a refait le tour du monde dans sa tête, se demandant quel endroit pourrait être le plus beau, le plus agréable et le plus intéressant pour lui après la vente de son bateau. Et cet homme qui connaissait vraiment la planète entière s'est rapidement décidé pour le Sud de l'Afrique. Il ne l'a jamais regretté.

Aujourd'hui, dans ce somptueux ouvrage, il nous fait redécouvrir ce continent mystérieux et magique dans de magnifiques photos. Qu'il en soit remercié ! Dommage que les Poliza ne soient pas plus nombreux en ce monde !

Florian Langenscheidt

Associé du groupe d'édition Langenscheidt et auteur de nombreux livres, Florian Langenscheidt est membre du Conseil de fondation du World-Wide Fund for Nature (WWF) et membre du Chairman's Council du Museum of Modern Art de New York.

Voyages de découverte

En l'an 2000, j'ai reçu une série de courriers électroniques en provenance d'un bateau nommé « STARSHIP » qui sillonnait les océans du monde, dans le cadre d'une expédition de trois ans pour la cause de l'environnement. Ces messages m'annonçaient qu'une partie de l'équipage aimerait visiter quelques-unes des plus belles réserves du Sud de l'Afrique.

Pour un premier safari, j'ai organisé à l'intention de Michael Poliza et d'une partie de son équipage la visite du delta de l'Okavango, au Botswana. Il est aussitôt tombé sous le charme de ce merveilleux pays, de sa faune et de ses habitants. Entre nous, le courant est passé. Après avoir mené son projet à terme, Michael est venu me voir à mon bureau et nous sommes partis ensemble à la découverte. Je l'ai conduit dans quelques endroits parmi les plus sauvages et les plus fascinants de la planète – et nous, véritables dinosaures sur le plan de la technique, il nous a initiés à la photographie et à la technologie numériques.

Michael a apporté une nouvelle perspective dans la photographie des animaux sauvages. Beaucoup de ses photographies d'animaux rendent obsolètes les règles généralement admises en matière de photographie de la vie sauvage. Il a réussi, par exemple, à saisir dans un gros plan tout le caractère du majestueux roi des lions, tout en désobéissant à ces règles et en ne montrant pas ses yeux.

Il a saisi l'essence de ces magnifiques paysages et de sa faune étonnante dans un style qui lui est bien propre. Il a introduit un regard nouveau, plus artistique, dans la photographie des animaux sauvages. Beaucoup de ses photos représentent les animaux d'une manière inconnue pour moi jusqu'alors. Un angle différent, très fermé, ou un effet très graphique, il devait souvent attendre des heures et des jours pour obtenir exactement cette image-là. Il ne semblait jamais fatigué de répéter ses tentatives, inlassablement, persuadé qu'il devait pouvoir réaliser là une photo encore meilleure.

Michael a inspiré un grand nombre de nos guides, membres de nos équipes et visiteurs à devenir de meilleurs photographes. Et nous, en notre qualité d'entreprise, il nous a inspirés à progresser et à nous perfectionner.

Colin Bell

Colin Bell est un véritable pionnier de l'industrie africaine du safari et un écologiste convaincu. Avec ses Wilderness Safaris camps, il a donné une qualité nouvelle à l'aventure du safari en Afrique. Il a reçu, au nom de l'équipe de Wilderness Safaris, de nombreux prix de l'environnement parmi les plus renommés, avant de se tourner, début 2006, vers de nouveaux challenges.

Acerca del fotógrafo

Michael Poliza es un Marco Polo del nuevo milenio. Primero, como empresario, acercó el mundo digital a Alemania. Y luego, emprendió él mismo una vuelta al mundo en mil días –en busca de los puntos más bellos y en mayor peligro de nuestro planeta, siguiendo las huellas de los antiguos exploradores.

Pero no lo hizo dotado de su mochila y cheques de viajero, sino de un barco especialmente diseñado al efecto, cargado hasta la gola de equipamiento técnico y mediático. Y todo ello acompañado de prudentes consideraciones económicas, es decir que el proyecto fue financiado por patrocinadores internacionales de peso. El libro y el DVD que resultaron de este viaje incomparable acercaron el mundo a decenas de miles de personas desde una perspectiva totalmente nueva.

Finalmente, Poliza emprendió una vuelta al mundo en su mente, tratando de elucidar qué sitio sería el más bello, el mejor, el más cautivador para él, una vez que hubiese vendido su barco. Y este viajero, de quien en verdad se puede afirmar que ya lo conocía todo, se inclinó muy rápidamente por el sur de África, una decisión que jamás lamentó.

Y ahora nos proporciona una nueva visión de este enigmático y mágico continente a través del magnífico tomo presente, con sus fantásticas imágenes. ¡Gracias! ¡Qué pena que sólo haya un Poliza en este mundo!

Florian Langenscheidt

Florian Langenscheidt, socio del grupo editorial Langenscheidt y autor de numerosos libros, es miembro del patronato de World-Wide Fund for Nature (WWF) y miembro del Chairman's Council en el Museo de Arte Moderno de Nueva York.

Viajes de exploración

En el año 2000 recibí una serie de mensajes por correo electrónico enviados desde el "STARSHIP", un barco que estaba dando la vuelta al mundo en una expedición de tres años bajo el signo de la concienciación medioambiental. En uno de ellos decían que una parte de la tripulación deseaba visitar algunos de los más bellos parques naturales del sur de África.

Durante nuestro primer safari, organicé una visita al delta del Okavango, en Botswana, para Michael Poliza y una parte de su tripulación. De inmediato, el encanto de este país maravilloso, de su mundo animal y de sus habitantes captaron la atención de Michael. El vínculo estaba establecido. Cuando finalizó su proyecto, volvió a visitarme en mi oficina, y salimos juntos de expedición. Lo conduje a algunos de los sitios más vírgenes y fascinantes de nuestro planeta, y él, por su parte, nos inició en el mundo de la fotografía y tecnología digitales: hasta ese momento, nosotros habíamos estado completamente apartados de las modernas tecnologías.

Michael introdujo una nueva perspectiva en la fotografía de animales salvajes; muchas de sus imágenes abandonan las reglas generales de la fotografía de la vida silvestre. Por ejemplo, consiguió plasmar la esencia del mayestático Rey León en una fotografía de primer plano a pesar de no ceñirse a las reglas de mostrar los ojo del felino.

Michael captó la esencia de estos magníficos paisajes y su fascinante mundo animal en un estilo muy propio, y aportó una visión novedosa, más artística, en la fotografía de animales salvajes. En muchas de sus imágenes, los animales se ven retratados de un modo totalmente nuevo para mí: ángulos diferentes, tomas de gran cercanía o muy gráficas. Con frecuencia, debió esperar horas para lograr precisamente esa imagen específica. Jamás dio la impresión de que se cansara al intentarlo una y otra vez, convencido de que siempre lo aguardaba una imagen aún mejor.

Michael ha inspirado a muchos de nuestros guías, empleados y visitantes a convertirse en mejores fotógrafos. Y, como empresarios, nos ha inspirado a avanzar y mejorar.

Colin Bell

Colin Bell es un verdadero precursor de la "industria" africana de los safaris y ecologista por convicción. Redefinió la experiencia del safari en África gracias a sus campamentos en Wilderness Safaris. En nombre de su magnífico equipo de Wilderness Safaris, recibió varios de los más preciados galardones mundiales del ámbito ecologista antes de entregarse a nuevos desafíos a comienzos de 2006.

Il fotografo

Michael Poliza è un Marco Polo a cavallo dei millenni. Prima, da imprenditore, ha aperto alla Germania l'accesso al mondo del digitale. Poi egli stesso è partito per un viaggio del mondo in mille giorni – alla ricerca dei luoghi più belli e a rischio del pianeta, sulle orme degli antichi esploratori.

Ma non armato di zaino e assegni di viaggio, bensì con una nave costruita appositamente, piena fino all'orlo di tecnica, di strumenti mediatici. E con ragionevole competenza in fatto di economia, vale a dire finanziato da grossi sponsor in tutto il mondo. Il libro e il DVD su questo viaggio straordinario hanno rivelato a decine di migliaia di persone un mondo nuovo.

Poi ha percorso col pensiero tutto il mondo, riflettendo su quale potesse essere per lui in futuro il luogo più bello, il migliore, il più interessante, dopo la vendita della nave. E, conoscendo davvero tutto, ha optato velocemente per l'Africa del Sud. Non se n'è mai pentito.

E ora, con questo magnifico volume, ci prende per mano, facendoci riscoprire con immagini grandiose questo continente misterioso e magico. Grazie di tutto ciò! Peccato che non ce ne siano di più come Poliza a questo mondo!

Florian Langenscheidt

Florian Langenscheidt, socio del gruppo editoriale Langenscheidt e autore di numerosi libri, è membro del consiglio della fondazione del World-Wide Fund for Nature (WWF) e membro del Chairman's Council del Museum of Modern Art di New York.

Viaggi di esplorazione

Nel 2000 ho ricevuto una serie di email da una nave di nome "STARSHIP", in viaggio intorno al mondo per una spedizione della durata di tre anni all'insegna della coscienza ecologica. C'era scritto che dei membri dell'equipaggio volevano visitare alcune tra le riserve più belle dell'Africa meridionale.

Nel nostro primo safari ho organizzato per Michael Poliza e una parte del suo equipaggio una visita nel delta dell'Okavango in Botswana. Fu subito stregato dal fascino di quel paese meraviglioso, dai suoi animali e i suoi abitanti. Si era già stabilito un rapporto. Michael mi venne a trovare in ufficio, dopo aver concluso il suo progetto, e andammo insieme in esplorazione. Lo portai in alcuni tra i luoghi più incontaminati e affascinanti di questo pianeta, e lui fece conoscere a noi, così digiuni di tecnica, il mondo della fotografia e della tecnologia digitale.

Michael ha introdotto un nuovo punto di vista nella fotografia degli animali selvaggi. Molte delle sue foto di animali scavalcano le regole generali della fotografia naturalistica. È stato in grado di catturare per intero, con un primo piano, l'indole del maestoso re leone, pur non mostrandone gli occhi e infrangendo così le regole.

Michael ha colto la sostanza di questi magnifici paesaggi e della loro fauna spettacolare secondo uno stile del tutto originale. Con lui la fotografia naturalistica si è appropriata di un punto di vista nuovo, più propriamente artistico. Molte delle sue foto sono ritratti di animali come non li avevo mai visti prima. Un'altra angolazione, ripresa molto da vicino o in maniera molto grafica – spesso ha dovuto attendere per ore e giornate intere, per ottenere esattamente quella determinata foto. Sembrava non stancarsi mai di continuare a riprovarci, nella convinzione che da qualche parte là fuori ci doveva essere un'immagine ancora più bella.

Michael ha ispirato molti tra i nostri dipendenti, tra le guide e i visitatori, a diventare fotografi migliori. E come compagnia ci ha stimolato ad andare avanti e a migliorare.

Colin Bell

Colin Bell è un vero pioniere dell'industria africana dei safari e un convinto ecologista. Con i suoi campi di Wilderness Safaris l'esperienza del safari in Africa ha acquistato una qualità nuova. A nome del team di Wilderness Safaris ha preso in consegna molti tra i più celebri premi per l'ambiente, prima di decidersi, nel 2006, ad affrontare compiti nuovi.

Thanks

The last four years have been extremely rewarding for me. Never in my life could I have imagined that I would be able to spend six or seven months a year in the bush—traveling by foot and by Land Rover. Never would I have dreamed of exploring the most remote and beautiful areas of this great continent, nor that I would be able to photograph the best Africa has to offer.

I have met so many amazing people and incredible guides who have been willing to share their enormous knowledge and show me their world. So, my greatest thanks go to: Brandon Kemp, Deborah White, Garth Thompson, Gregg Hughes, Dave Luck, Richard Cook, Mike Myers, Lee Whittam, Benson Siyawareva, Tendai Mdluli, Humphrey Gumpo, Map Ives and the late Nandi Retiyo, as well as to Copper Malela, Brooks Kamanakoa, Mr. T, Peace, Tsile Tsile and Francis, to name but a few. Thanks, guys! Without you, all of this would never have been possible, so this book is dedicated to you!

But there are many more people to thank: David Bristow, for introducing me to Colin Bell, and Colin for showing me some of the greatest wildlife areas on this planet and for welcoming me into Wilderness Safaris Camps. Many thanks as well to: Malcolm McCulloch, Andy Payne, Russel Friedman, Dave van Smeerdijk, Keith Vincent, Grant Woodrow, Rob Moffett, Bruce Simpson, Mike Wassung, Craig Higgins, Trudi Waggott, Cate Procter, Mari Dos Santos, Lizzy Bayane and Tana Hutchings for putting up with all my requests. The Sefofane pilots and team for dealing with my extra luggage on board the small bush planes. Wolfgang Rapp, who tragically died in a plane crash in Dec 2006, for being a hell of a pilot and patient enough to deal with me. Stefano Cheli, Justin Grammaticas and Andrea Maggi for introducing me to East Africa.

And, of course, thanks go to my great, long-time friends Tom Jacobi and Eric Locke, who taught me a thing or two about photography: Eric for sharing his against-the-light theory, and Tom for his clean and aesthetic principles. And I must not forget to mention Stephan Schröter and Axel Ohm, for always being there when I needed them.

Last but by no means least, I would like to thank Sabine Raab for sharing my passion for the bush. She was around and supported me tremendously while many of these images were taken.

Thanks to you all (and especially those I've forgotten to mention!).

A further comment: All of the images in this book were shot with CANON digital cameras and are real photographs. Nothing has been added or manipulated, apart from the normal fine-tuning of contrast, brightness and color. Also, no animals or people were harassed, harmed or killed while the pictures in this book were being taken. All of the photographs were shot in unfenced areas in the wild.

Michael Poliza

Dear Reader,
If you are enjoying these images, please visit my website www.michaelpoliza.com. You will find a wealth of images, a slideshow, screensaver and lots more information on the individual shots. Please check it out!

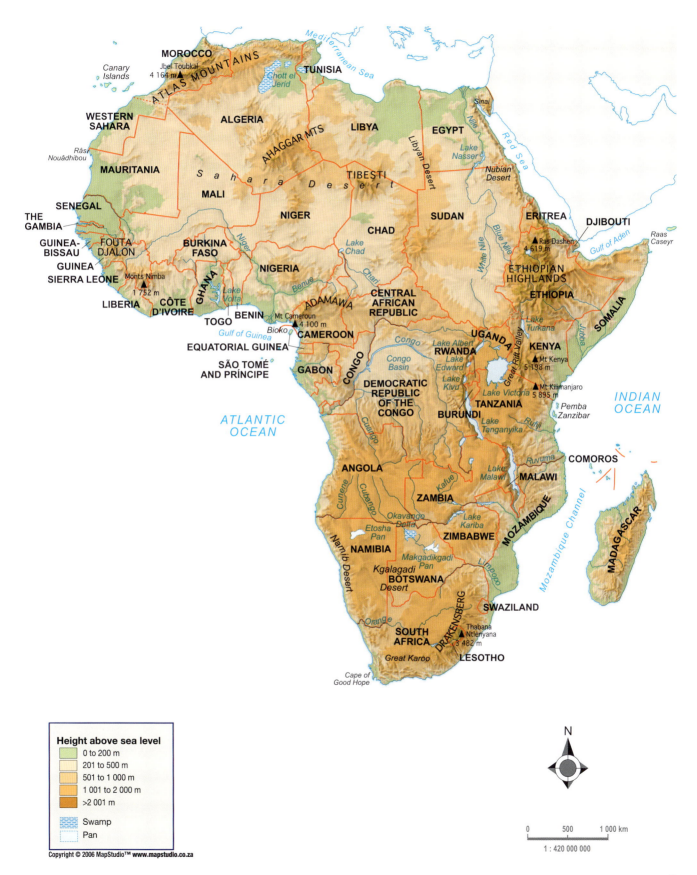

MOROCCO

Canary
Islands

Jbel Toubkal
4 164 m▲

ATLAS MOUNTAINS

TUNISIA

Mediterranean Sea

Chott el
Jerid

WESTERN
SAHARA

ALGERIA

AHAGGAR MTS

LIBYA

EGYPT

Sinai

Nile

Red Sea

Râs
Nouâdhibou

MAURITANIA

Sahara Desert

TIBESTI

Libyan Desert

Lake
Nasser

Nubian
Desert

MALI

NIGER

CHAD

SUDAN

ERITREA

Ras Dashen
4 619 m▲

DJIBOUTI

Gulf of Aden

Raas
Caseyr

SENEGAL

THE
GAMBIA

GUINEA-
BISSAU

GUINEA

SIERRA LEONE

LIBERIA

FOUTA
DJALON

Niger

BURKINA
FASO

NIGERIA

Lake
Chad

Chari

White Nile

Blue Nile

ETHIOPIAN
HIGHLANDS

Monts Nimba
1 752 m▲

GHANA

CÔTE
D'IVOIRE

Lake
Volta

TOGO

BENIN

Benue

ADAMAWA

CENTRAL
AFRICAN
REPUBLIC

ETHIOPIA

SOMALIA

Lake
Turkana

Jubba

Mt Cameroun
4 100 m▲

Bioko

Gulf of Guinea

CAMEROON

EQUATORIAL GUINEA

SÃO TOMÉ
AND PRÍNCIPE

GABON

CONGO

Congo

Congo
Basin

Lake Albert

Lake
Edward

Lake
Kivu

UGANDA

RWANDA

BURUNDI

Great Rift Valley

KENYA

Mt Kenya
5 198 m▲

Mt Kilimanjaro
5 895 m▲

Lake Victoria

TANZANIA

Pemba
Zanzibar

INDIAN
OCEAN

ATLANTIC
OCEAN

DEMOCRATIC
REPUBLIC
OF THE
CONGO

Cuango

Lake
Tanganyika

Rufiji

Ruvuma

COMOROS

ANGOLA

Kafue

Lake
Malawi

MALAWI

MOZAMBIQUE

Mozambique Channel

Cunene

Cubango

ZAMBIA

Okavango
Delta

Lake
Kariba

MADAGASCAR

Etosha
Pan

ZIMBABWE

Namib Desert

NAMIBIA

Makgadikgadi
Pan

Limpopo

Kgalagadi
Desert

BOTSWANA

DRAKENSBERG

SWAZILAND

Orange

Thabana
Ntlenyana
3 482 m▲

SOUTH
AFRICA

Great Karoo

LESOTHO

Cape of
Good Hope

Height above sea level

0 to 200 m
201 to 500 m
501 to 1 000 m
1 001 to 2 000 m
>2 001 m

Swamp
Pan

N

0   500   1 000 km

1 : 420 000 000

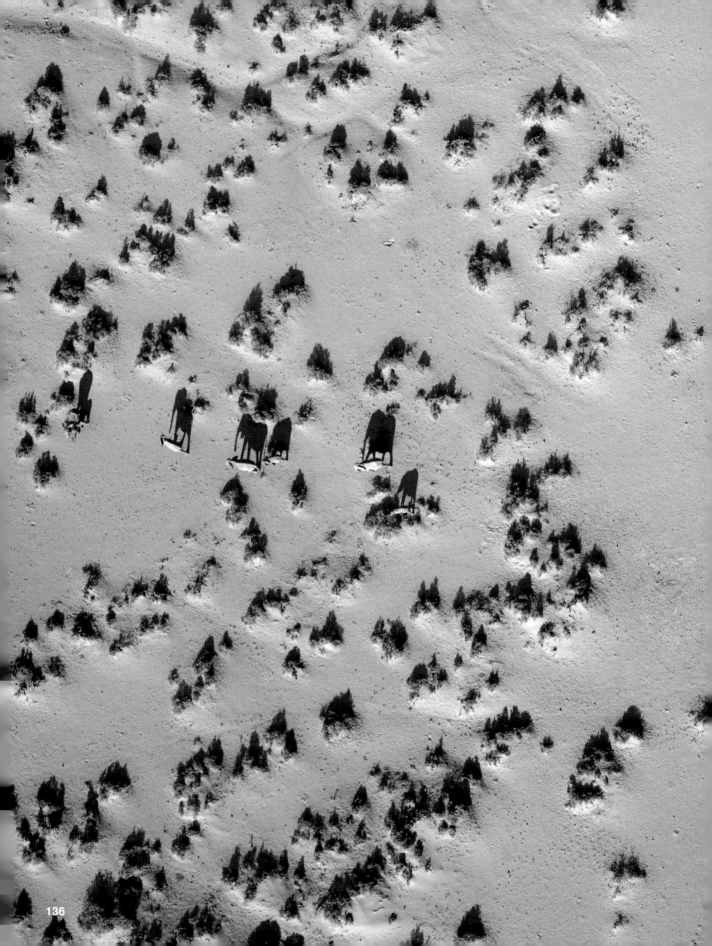

INDEX

Second Edition

© 2008 teNeues Verlag GmbH + Co. KG, Kempen
© 2008 Michael Poliza

Photographs by Michael Poliza

Preface by Florian Langenscheidt
Journey of Discovery by Colin Bell

Translations by Werkstatt München / Martin Waller:
English: Louisa Schaefer and Jon Smale
German: Martin Waller (Colin Bell)
French: Dominique Kirmer
Spanish: Gladys Janicha
Italian: Maria Teresa Arbia

Layout:
Robert Kuhlendahl, Axel Theyhsen, teNeues Verlag
Editorial coordination:
Sabine Wagner, Arndt Jasper, teNeues Verlag
Production: Sandra Jansen, teNeues Verlag

Color separation by Medien Team-Vreden, Germany

Published by teNeues Publishing Group

teNeues Verlag GmbH + Co. KG
Am Selder 37
47906 Kempen, Germany
Phone: 0049-(0)2152-916-0
Fax: 0049-(0)2152-916-111
e-mail: books@teneues.de

Press department: arehn@teneues.de
Phone: 0049-(0)2152-916-202

teNeues Publishing Company
16 West 22nd Street
New York, NY 10010, USA
Phone: 001-212-627-9090
Fax: 001-212-627-9511

teNeues Publishing UK Ltd.
P.O. Box 402
West Byfleet
KT14 7ZF, Great Britain
Phone: 0044-(0)1932-40 35 09
Fax: 0044-(0)1932-40 35 14

teNeues France S.A.R.L.
4, rue de Valence
75005 Paris, France
Phone: 0033-(0)1-55 76-62 05
Fax: 0033-(0)1-55 76-64 19

www.teneues.com

While we strive for utmost precision in every detail,
we cannot be held responsible for any inaccuracies,
neither for any subsequent loss or damage arising.

Bibliographic information published by Die Deutsche
Bibliothek. Die Deutsche Bibliothek lists this publication in
the Deutsche Nationalbibliografie; detailed bibliographic
data is available in the Internet at http://dnb.ddb.de.

ISBN: 978-3-8327-9197-1

Printed in Italy

teNeues Publishing Group
Kempen
Düsseldorf
Hamburg
London
Madrid
Milan
Munich
New York
Paris

teNeues